A GIFT OF Inspiration for a Mother's Heart

Stories for the Heart *Mini* Books

COMPILED *by* ALICE GRAY

A Gift of Inspiration for a Mother's Heart
a Stories for the Heart Mini Book

© 2002 by Multnomah Publishers, Inc.
published by Multnomah Gifts™, a division of Multnomah® Publishers, Inc.
P.O. Box 1720, Sisters, Oregon 97759

ISBN 1-59052-027-0

Designed by Koechel Peterson & Associates, Minneapolis, Minnesota

Multnomah Publishers, Inc., has made every effort to
trace the ownership of all poems and quotes.
In the event of a question arising from the use of a poem or quote,
we regret any error made and will be pleased to make the
necessary correction in future editions of this book.

Please see the acknowledgments at the back of the book
for complete attributions for this material.

Scripture quotations are taken from *The Holy Bible*,
New International Version © 1973, 1984 by International Bible Society,
used by permission of Zondervan Publishing House.

Multnomah is a trademark of Multnomah Publishers, Inc.,
and is registered in the U.S. Patent and Trademark Office.
The colophon is a trademark of Multnomah Publishers, Inc.

All rights reserved. No portion of this book may be reproduced
in any form without the written permission of the publisher.

Printed in China

02 03 04 05 06 07 08 — 10 9 8 7 6 5 4 3 2 1 0

www.multnomahgifts.com

Table of Contents

Just the Right Size by Rev. Morris Chalfant — 8

Love on Me by Becky Freeman — 12

Look at All Those Weeds by Cindy Rosene Deadrick — 16

Mother Won't Let Me by Caroline Brownlow — 24

Love Notes by Dale Hanson Bourke — 26

Somebody's Mother by Mary Dow Brine — 32

The Spirit of Hospitality by Emilie Barnes — 36

I Was Chosen by Susan Alexander Yates and Allison Yates Gaskins — 42

Bedtime — 50

She Held His Hand by Carla Muir — 52

The Nest by Evelyn Petty — 54

Just the Right Size

Rev. Morris Chalfant

It was the day before Mother's Day that a little boy, money tightly clutched in his hand, came to a department store to make a purchase. Bashfully he approached a woman clerk. "I want to buy a present for Mom." Then embarrassed, he added, "A slip."

"What size does she wear?"

He hesitated, "I don't know anything about sizes."

"Is she tall? Short? Large? Small?"

The lad was ready to answer. "Mother is just right!" He was so firm about it that the lady clerk wrapped up a size 36. The following Monday, the boy's mother returned to the store with the slip and exchanged it for a size 52! Size meant nothing to the lad; his mother had won his heart!

No language can express the power and beauty and heroism and majesty of a mother's love.

E.H. CHAPIN

What Really Matters

One hundred years from now
it will not matter
what kind of car I drove,
what kind of house I lived in,
how much money I had
in my bank account,
nor what my clothes looked like.
But one hundred years from now
the world may be a little better
because I was important
in the life of a child.

AUTHOR UNKNOWN

Love on Me

Becky Freeman

I'd delayed as long as I could. It was time to stop by the school library to complete records for my three school-age children.

Why the procrastination?

Take four children, numerous shots per child, and an absent-minded mother who had no idea where she'd filed "Children's Immunizations." Fortunately, I looked under "T" for "Traumatic Experiences." Locating birth certificates was equally challenging.

I asked the school secretary if I could just show her my stretch marks as proof of my children's births. By the time I had finished filling out forms, I was so tired I put "undecided" in the blank next to "name" and "not applicable" in the blank beside "sex."

My preschooler, Gabe, who'd come along on this errand, was remarkably quiet. When I looked up, I saw the reason: He'd been happily licking and sticking postage stamps to the library shelves.

A half hour later, shelves de-stamped, I scooped Gabe into my arms and dashed for the car muttering, "Gabe, Momma's got to stop by the store and clean the house and…" Lowering him into the car seat, I felt his arms tighten around my shoulders and his warm breath on my neck. "And love on me," he whispered.

I felt as if I'd been running at top speed and had hit a wire stretched across the road. Looking into Gabriel's upturned face, I brushed his soft, dark hair from his forehead, grateful for a three-year-old with clear-cut priorities.

"Yes," I answered as I hugged him closely, "and most importantly, love on you."

Look at All Those Weeds

Cindy Rosene Deadrick

"Beauty is in the eye of the beholder," as the old saying goes, and so I am reminded by my three-year-old daughter as she erupts into screams of delight at the sight of our front yard abloom with a multitude of riotous dandelions. "Sunflowers!" she shouts. Eagerly, she recruits her two-year-old sister to assist in gathering a bouquet for Mom. Hand in hand, they dash about the yard, hardly knowing where to start, each sunny blossom as enticing as the next. After several minutes they return, each clutching a handful of twisted stems with golden heads, which they thrust into my reluctant palm.

"Put them on your desk, Mommy—in a cup of water in case they get thirsty," my preschooler instructs me. I don't have the heart to tell my daughters that their newfound treasures are only present on our lawn because their father applied the wrong kind of weed killer.

"I bet there'll be lots more when we come home tonight," she tells me, unable to contain her excitement. She has no idea just how many hundreds more will appear. Certainly dandelions have a way of multiplying that defies logic. Indeed, our entire two-acre lot will soon be awash in a yellow sea, not a blade of grass visible to the eye, and our usually friendly neighbors will be secretly scorning us for contaminating the entire block with the invasive yellow flowers. The county Weed Board will probably want us to be the poster family in their "Control Obnoxious Weeds" campaign.

Over the course of the next week, my two darlings continue to delight in their morning garden-tending duties, beginning each day with a dandelion-picking session and happily bestowing their floral gifts on a succession of their favorite people: Daddy, Grandma, their day-care provider—even the family mutt. His kennel has never looked better than it does now, graced with a flurry of canary-colored blooms.

As we drive through town going about our daily routine, our car is filled with shouts of glee as my little Dandelion Patrol Girls spy yet another yard filled with the glorious golden interloper. Elated at their good fortune in finding still more of the wondrous weed, they beg me to stop and let them gather a few more stems.

In their infinite capacity to simply enjoy life, my two young offspring gradually bring me to an attitude adjustment. "Why not take time to stop and pick the dandelions?" I finally ask myself. Who dictated that humans shouldn't enjoy certain varieties of flowers unless they are properly contained? It was probably the idea of some chemical company seeking to increase sales. But the joy we take in a jolt of vibrant color after a long, gray winter shouldn't be diminished just because some unknown arbiter of landscape fashion has decreed that a blush of gold spoils the look of a well-groomed lawn.

So, while my husband is consulting with the chemical expert at our local lawn and garden center, trying to determine what went awry in his carefully conceived weed-control plan, I have joined in the fun with my daughters. My workday is brightened by five lemony blooms winking at me from a small jar on my desk, and I have a renewed, childlike appreciation for the natural beauty all around me. I am determined to slow down and take notice of all the simple pleasures nature has in store. The other day when my daughter filled her pocket with shiny pebbles she found in the driveway, she told me she found diamonds. And I believed her.

Love is not blind;

love sees a great deal more

than the actual.

Love sees the ideas,

the potential in us.

OSWALD CHAMBERS

Mother Won't Let Me

Caroline Brownlow

A policeman noticed a boy with a lot of stuff packed on his back riding a tricycle around and around the block.

Finally, he asked the boy where he was going.

"I'm running away from home," the boy said.

The policeman then asked him, "Why do you keep going around and around the block?"

The boy answered, "My mother won't let me cross the street."

Love Notes

Dale Hanson Bourke

"*So you're* the one who started all the trouble!" the well-dressed woman said to me as I introduced myself. I looked at her blankly. Standing in the middle of our children's classroom, I couldn't imagine what she was talking about.

"The notes," she declared. "I mean the notes in the children's lunchboxes. Because of your son, all the children have to have them now."

My mouth dropped open as I listened to her. I had no idea anyone even knew about the notes I tucked into Chase's lunchbox each day. But apparently he had shown them to his friends, who asked their mothers for notes, too.

I usually did my son's notes late at night before I fell into bed, or early in the morning before anyone else was awake. Blurry-eyed, I drew pictures or wrote simple words that Chase would recognize. These communiqués were my way of helping him make it through his long school day. So at lunchtime I tried to give him a little extra boost to remind him that he was special.

Now I realized the notes *had* made a difference for Chase. He felt so good about them that he had shown them to his friends. And they all wanted to feel special as well.

Each night when I cleaned out Chase's lunchbox, I would find the day's note, with greasy little fingerprints on it. It made me smile to think of him reading his note each day as he ate his lunch.

One day I opened his lunchbox to find only crumbs and a half-eaten carrot. "Where's your note, Chase?" I asked.

He looked sheepish. "Sorry, Mom," he said. "I gave it to Jimmy."

"Why?"

"Well, he never gets a note. So I thought I could share mine with him." Chase looked at me sideways, waiting for my reaction.

He was relieved when I bent down and hugged him. Jimmy's mom was single and worked long hours to support her family. I was proud my son passed his precious note on to Jimmy.

"You're a very special boy," I told him.

"I know," he responded.

All I could do was laugh. I had thought that Chase needed a note each day to remind him of that fact. Instead, he was reminding his classmates through his kindness. More importantly, he was reminding me.

The future destiny

of a child is always

the work of a mother.

NAPOLEON

Somebody's Mother

The woman was old and ragged and gray
And bent with the chill of the winter's day.

The street was wet with a recent snow
And the woman's feet were aged and slow.

She stood at the crossing and waited long,
Alone, uncared for, amid the throng

Of human beings who passed her by
Nor heeded the glance of her anxious eye.

Down the street, with laughter and shout,

Glad in the freedom of "school let out,"

Came the boys like a flock of sheep,

Hailing the snow piled white and deep,

Past the woman so old and gray

Hastened the children on their way.

Nor offered a helping hand to her—

So meek, so timid, afraid to stir

Lest the carriage wheels or the horse's feet

Should crowd her down in the slippery street.

At last came one of the merry troop,

The gladest laddie of all the group;

He paused beside her and whispered low,

"I'll help you cross, if you wish to go."

Her aged hand on his strong young arm

She placed, and so, without hurt or harm,

He guided the trembling feet along,

Proud that his own were firm and strong.

Then back again to his friends he went,

His young heart happy and well content.

"She's somebody's mother, boys, you know,

For all she's aged and poor and slow,
And I hope some fellow will lend a hand
To help my mother, you understand,
If ever she's poor and old and gray,
When her own dear boy is far away."
And "somebody's mother" bowed low her head
In her home that night, and the prayer she said
Was, "God be kind to the noble boy,
Who is somebody's son, and pride and joy!"

MARY DOW BRINE

The Spirit of Hospitality

Emilie Barnes

The "parlor" was tiny, just an extra room behind the store. But the tablecloth was spotless; the candles were glowing; the flowers were bright; the tea was fragrant. Most of all, the smile was genuine and welcoming whenever my mother invited people to "come on back for a cup of tea."

How often I heard her say those words when I was growing up. And how little I realized the mark they would make on me.

Those were hard years after my father died, when Mama and I shared three rooms behind her little dress shop. Mama waited on the customers, did alterations, and worked on the books until late at night. I kept house—planning and shopping for meals, cooking, cleaning, doing laundry—while going to school and learning the dress business as well.

Sometimes I felt like Cinderella—work, work, work. And the little girl in me longed for a Prince Charming to carry me away to his castle. There I would preside over a grand and immaculate household, waited on hand and foot by attentive servants. I would wear gorgeous dresses and entertain kings and queens who marveled at my beauty and my wisdom and brought me lavish gifts.

But in the meantime, of course, I had work to do. And although I didn't know it, I was already receiving a gift more precious than any dream castle could be. For unlike Cinderella, I lived with a loving mama who understood the true meaning of sharing and joy—a mama who brightened people's lives with the spirit of hospitality.

Our customers quickly learned that Mama offered a sympathetic ear as well as elegant clothes and impeccable service. Often they ended up sharing their hurts and problems with her. And then, inevitably, would come the invitation: "Let me make you a cup of tea." She would usher our guests back to our main room, which served as a living room by day and a bedroom by night. Quickly a fresh cloth was slipped on the table, a candle lit, fresh flowers set out if possible, and the teapot heated. If we had them, she would pull out cookies or a loaf of banana bread. There was never anything fancy, but the gift of her caring warmed many a heart on a cold night.

My mama's willingness to open her life to

others—to share her home, her food, and her love—was truly a royal gift. She passed it along to me, and I have the privilege of passing it on to others. What a joy to be part of the spirit of hospitality!

I want to be like you—
a well-watered garden
whose fragrance causes all around
to breath in...
deeply.

KIMBER ANNIE ENGSTROM

I Was Chosen

Susan Alexander Yates
and Allison Yates Gaskins

It was time for bed and I really didn't mind too much. It meant Mommy would smooth my sheets and crawl in my bed with me. I'd snuggle in her arms and she'd rub my hair and tell me how special I was and how much she loved me. If it wasn't too late and Mommy wasn't too tired, I might get to hear The Story before we said our prayers together.

I never grew tired of hearing her tell The Story. It was so special because it was about me. I was an only child and I was adopted. Mommy would begin by saying, "Your daddy and I always wanted a baby. We wanted one for so long, and we kept praying that I would get pregnant and have a baby. But after several years when I didn't get pregnant, we began to realize that God had something even better for us. He decided that He was going to give us a very special baby—a baby that another lady was not able to take care of. He wanted parents who would be just right for this very special baby. Guess who that very special baby was? You!"

"Mommy, tell me about the day you got me."

"Well, Tucker," she would continue, "That was the most exciting day in my life! It began when the telephone rang, and a voice on the other end said, 'Mrs. Freeman, your beautiful little baby girl has just been born. Would you like to come see her?'

"I called your daddy at the office and he raced home and got me and we hurried to the hospital. At first we stood outside the window where all the new babies were and just looked at them, trying to figure out which one was you! When we got to the end of the row of babies, there you were and you turned your head and looked at us and seemed to smile!

"We couldn't wait to take you home and

introduce you to our family and friends. When we drove up in front of our house, there were lots of friends who had come to see you and to bring you presents! You have always been such a gift to us. Why, the smartest thing Daddy and I ever did in our lives was adopt you!"

Each time Mother told me The Story she got excited. She never tired of telling it, and I never got tired of hearing her tell it. From the beginning she made me feel that being adopted was tremendously special, that I had somehow been chosen.

When I was about seven months pregnant

with my own child, my mother came to visit. It was one of those really uncomfortable days, and the baby was kicking nonstop. As I groaned and held my stomach, my mother said, "It must be amazing to feel her kick."

Suddenly, it dawned on me that my mother had never felt a baby inside her womb.

"Mother," I said, "come and put your hands on my stomach. I want you to feel your grandchild."

The look of awe on my mother's face as she felt her granddaughter kick in the womb was so precious for me. I realized that I was able to give my mother a gift she had not been able to experience personally. She had given me so many gifts, and finally I was able to share a very personal one with her.

*It was when I had
my first child
that I understood
how much my
mother loved me.*

AUTHOR UNKNOWN

The angels, *whispering*

to one another,

can find among

their burning terms of *love,*

none so devotional as that of *mother.*

EDGAR ALLAN POE

Bedtime

Author unknown

After putting her children to bed, a mother changed into old slacks and a droopy blouse and proceeded to wash her hair. As she heard the children getting more and more rambunctious, her patience grew thin. At last she threw a towel around her head and stormed into their room, putting them back to bed with stern warnings. As she left the room, she heard her three-year-old say with a trembling voice, "Who was that?"

She Held His Hand

She held his hand when he was born

one sunlit April day.

She held his hand first day of school

then bravely drove away.

She held his hand and battled fears

above and under bed.

She held his hand then gave a kiss

before her son was wed.

She held his hand as on he bragged
through newborn daughter's cry.
She held his hand as his girl waved
when graduates passed by.
Yet it was he who held her hand
and watched her soul depart.
Though he no longer holds her hand
he holds her in his heart.

CARLA MUIR

The Nest

Evelyn Petty

Our front door slammed open and shut many times over the years, but there was one summer it was silenced—the summer before the last of our three children left for college. Christine, John, and Jeff had been fun to raise and the delight of my life. Even the thought of them leaving home felt empty.

One day, I noticed a mother bird feverishly making a nest on the light fixture by our front door. Twigs and debris were scattered on the ground underneath. Somewhat anxious brown eyes peered quietly over the edge at me.

From that time forward, the front door was off limits. Through the entire active summer, with two kids home from college and another one preparing to leave, everyone used the kitchen door. Soon, the nest burst into activity with the arrival of three little birds. We were able to watch from the kitchen as the mother bird fed and fluffed her babies, cleaned out the nest, and eventually taught them to fly. And then one day, they were gone.

I thought about the mother bird and how her care and tending had ended as the birds flew away leaving nothing but a nest. From the moment I counted the three birds, I began identifying with the whole process, so I carefully took the abandoned home down from its perch and placed it on a shelf in the garage. As I watched Chris and John and now Jeff pack to leave home, I wept realizing the inevitable had come; I had raised my family and it was time for them to apply all the lessons home had taught them.

Late in October of the same year, an unusually loud thunderstorm hit our area. I looked out the kitchen window at the sky and a movement caught my eye. There, huddled under the eaves by the front door, near the porch light, were three fledgling birds. I'm sure it was "our family," returning to find shelter in the only place they knew for sure was safe, familiar, welcoming—because it was home.

Smiling, I returned to my breakfast, knowing I'd been given reassurance. Though the years of nurturing were over, the years ahead would bring many opportunities for sheltering our family. When the crisis, the frightening, the difficult, or the overwhelming times come, there is one place that will always be safe, familiar, welcoming for my family—home.

"Mother" means
selfless *devotion*,
limitless *sacrifice*,
and *love*
that passes understanding.

AUTHOR UNKNOWN

A mother's love is indeed
the golden link that binds youth to age;
and he is still but a child, however time
may have furrowed his cheek,
or slivered his brow, who can yet recall,
with a softened heart, the fond
devotion, or the gentle chidings, of
the best friend that God ever gives us.

CHRISTIAN BOVEE

All that I am,

or hope to be,

I owe to my mother.

ABRAHAM LINCOLN

Acknowledgments

"Just the Right Size" by Rev. Morris Chalfant. Used by permission of the author.

"Love on Me" by Becky Freeman, taken from *Seasons of a Woman's Heart*. © 1999. Becky Freeman is the bestselling author of many humorous books for women. Visit her bookshelf at www.beckyfreeman.com. Used by permission of the author.

"Look at All Those Weeds" by Cindy Rosene Deadrick. © 1998. Used by permission of Brownlow Corporation.

"Mother Won't Let Me" by Caroline Brownlow. © 1999. Used by permission of the author.

"Love Notes" by Dale Hanson Bourke. © 1989. Used by permission of the author.

"The Spirit of Hospitality" by Emilie Barnes, taken from *The Spirit of Loveliness*, by Emilie Barnes. © 1999 by Harvest House Publishers, Eugene, OR 97402. Used by permission.

"I Was Chosen" by Susan Alexander Yates and Allison Yates Gaskins. © 1997. Susan Alexander Yates is the author of *How to Like the Ones You Love: Building Family Friendships for Life*. Used by permission of the authors.

"She Held His Hand" by Carla Muir. © 1997. Used by permission of the author.

"The Nest" by Evelyn Petty. Used by permission of the author.